UNDER THE APPLE BOUGHS

For my wife Honor.
who knew the people and the places

and

To the memory of Laurie Lee

Under the Apple Boughs

A Journey through a West Country Year

Peter Maughan

THE HOBNOB PRESS

First published in 2013 by The Cluny Press

This edition published in 2020 by The Hobnob Press,
8 Lock Warehouse, Severn Road, Gloucester GL1 2GA
www.hobnobpress.co.uk

British Library Cataloguing in Publication Data
A catalogue record for this book is available from the British Library

ISBN 978-1-906978-90-7

Typeset in Doves Type 15/18 pt
Typesetting and origination by John Chandler

Front cover illustration by Angel Dominguez

CONTENTS

Now as I was young and easy under the apple boughs
About the lilting house and happy as the grass was green,
The night above the dingle starry,
Time let me hail and climb
Golden in the heydays of his eyes. . .

Fern Hill. Dylan Thomas

A YEAR'S BEGINNING

ALL NIGHT the vixen had screamed down the burning fields of frost, under a sky chiming with January stars, running under a moon and the wild white hair of trees. The barking of a dog fox led on and on across the valley in search of her, until their clamour died in the hot-throated distance and the pulse of the morning star dimmed like a weakening signal over the land.

The moon was full and sitting above the tall pines now, above the road that falls into the valley, its ringing light striking the blue frost-bright slate of the village, echoing down the headlong High Street, fading away into silences where the shadows had drifted, piled like soot.

The village crossed the border of two counties, high on a valley side, arranged as if by a child's hand around shop, church and pub. Only the light from the telephone box burned in the lampless High Street, shining with a busy toy redness outside the post office and shop.

From clear across the valley, a farm dog barked into the no-man's-land between night and morning, and a tawny owl glided across the village, its flight as silence and as remote as a dream.

Fluttering for a hold on top of a telegraph pole, it folded its wings, its blunt head moving in sweeps as it searched for small scurries of movement from shadow to shadow below, and finding none sang about it, the long-drawn, quavering notes sounding under the moon like a ghost story told to a child.

From the terrace of farm cottages in the High Street, a baby howled damply at the world, and a light came on in a bedroom, as the owl beat its way down through the village to the wood below, its swift, sharp call in flight a fingernail drawn across the frosted glass of dawn.

Other lights shone in the village now. In the post office and the shop where newspapers, hot from the London train, were sorted for the bin outside. In the kitchen of George Perry, coal merchant, waiting for the weather forecast and hoping for the worst. In the bedroom of Miss Holsworth, village spinster, dressing to the frivolous notes of a horn concerto on Radio 3.

And in the farmhouse at the top of the High Street, where breakfast steamed the windows, and the lights went on in the milking shed. Udders swinging, the hunched shadows of the cattle were herded from the stalls, the cobbles of the yard brittle with silver under the moon, the dung-heavy smell almost as warm as breath.

Bales of last season's hay in the Dutch barn were tossed down onto a trailer for the stock in the fields, sweetening the air briefly with the scent of an impossibly remote summer. The tractor headlights swept across the yards, petrifying a returning barn-hunting cat, and turning into the High Street, rode off the hill into the quenching dark of the valley.

Battered and cooling, the moon settled above the Norman tower of the church, the black and gold clock fingered with elegant shadows, a smell like damp burnt paper on the raw air as the first fires of the morning were lit. And from the farm in the High Street a cockcrow flared with sudden petulance, as if in protest at the cold and grudging dawn, its light spreading above the hills in the east like a stain.

Dug in across the farmlands the creatures of the day felt its tug, but in the weather that had sent the owl home early slept on as if waiting for spring. Rooks in the grounds of what was once the squire's house, stirred, moving in the tops of the horse chestnuts, preening and bickering. And in the wood below the village, pheasants scratched, squawking, for food, raucous with complaint at the ungiving earth, and pigeons broke through the trees with a clatter of wings, and turned blindly towards the fields.

Like the slow unclenching of a fist, the dawn gave up more light. A hard, clay-heavy light, worked into the sky as if with a palette knife. And birds sang, stray thin winter notes as the last of the night broke up over the valley, and the light above the hills gathered into a new day.

COLD COMFORT

OLD MR COMBES wiped at his mouth with a hand. He was hunched over his pint like a bowl of workhouse soup, his head half buried in his turned up overcoat collar. 'Crops stinking the whole bloody country out,' he went on, chewing the words damp with venom. 'Going to rot in the ground. And a war on.' His head slithered further out of his collar. 'So don't talk to I about the coldest bloody winter this century!' John Buttle shifted his huge bulk in the chair. 'That's as maybe, Mr Combes, and I'm sure that –' 'In 'seventy-nine –' Jim Howel started.

Young Wilf Perkin, who'd been to grammar school and was rumoured to have something to do with computers, coughed sharply, twice. 'I think you'll find,' he said, frowning with facts, 'that nineteen sixty three was the coldest winter this century. Indeed, if I'm not mistaken, it was the worse winter on record in central and southern England since the year seventeen forty.'

Mr Combes's brittle yellow eyes slid in Wilf's direction. 'Read that off the back of a matchbox, did you?' he sneered, and worked his false teeth up and down a couple of times nastily.

A week before, snow had been forecast. Snow was gathering in the north and would, by the weekend, come down on the West County like a fist. Extra food and fuel were ordered, sheep herded lower down the valley, and the bird table in the postmistress's garden was made up like the spare room.

But the threatened snow had not arrived. And that evening in the village pub, the Pike, the talk had scornfully left the present to dig up winters past, their iron ghosts sent clanking and blowing now around the small, log-warmed bar.

'In nineteen seventy-nine, the winter to which I referred,' Jim Howel said haughtily, ignoring Wilf and addressing the bald brown shell of Mr Combe's head, which had retreated again into his collar, 'the parish council were discussing using pneumatic drills to try and salvage some of the crops. Until it snowed, that is. Then you couldn't even see the tops of the hedges, never mind the fields. It was so bad there was talk of rationing, and bringing the army in. Oh, yes!' he insisted, as eyebrows went up around the bar.

Jim sat back, arms folded, and stared at the opposite wall like a small boy sticking to a tall story.

'Six of one and half dozen of the other, I've no doubt,' Mr Beesley said, showing his teeth in a vague placatory smile.

'Oh-ah!' George Perry said, and leered as if talking of women. George had a coal yard in the village and whistled at his shovel through all the windfalls of winter. 'Mind you, I don't know about digging up fields and the army coming in, and all that,' George went on, one eye on Jim Howel, 'but young Wilf here's right enough about 'sixty three. Me and dad had the snow chains on practically all that winter, that I do remember. 'Twere a shocker.'

'You must have had a bumpy bloody ride, then, ' Jim said. 'We never saw –'

'And if it weren't the snow,' George went on as if Jim hadn't spoken, 'then it were the diesel freezing up you. With a full load on the back. In the middle of nowhere, and with night coming on.'

Wilf Perkin, idly playing with an empty peanut bag in an ashtray, nodded in grim agreement.

'All that's as maybe,' John Buttle said fussily, stepping over two of the pub's dogs sprawled in front of the fire, 'but what about 'eighty-two? What about that lot, then?' he wanted to know, whistling the words as he bent his weight to beat a bit more life out of the logs with the poker.

He straightened up in stages and blew a couple of times, his face the color of bacon. 'That snow! I thought we'd never see the end of it.'

He sat down again, shuddering elaborately, and drawing from Mrs Beesley sitting opposite an equally elaborate grimace of sympathy.

Jim Howel looked angry. 'Some people have got a short memory. We were cut off here half the bloody winter in 'seven-nine.'

'From mid-January till the end of February, intermittently,' Wilf supplied.

Mrs Beesley leaned her ample body forward, the floral print dress with the buttons up the front bulging under the sudden avalanche of breasts like a parcel coming undone. 'They landed here in a helicopter then, and took June Fitch off pregnant,' she said, and sat back gratified.

'Who did?' Mr Beesley said with a worried expression.

'Probably an Air-Sea rescue job from Portland,' Wilf said, narrowing his eyes.

Jim Howel shifted impatiently in his seat.

Mrs Beesley nodded at Wilf. 'That year, it was. Nineteen sixty-three. When we were cut off with the snow. A week overdue June were, and her husband saying not to worry, she'll calve down when she's ready.' Mrs Beesley moved the handbag on her lap in agitation.

Jim Howel opened his mouth to speak.

'And it were just after that that the poor old Pool sisters died,' Mrs Beesley suddenly remembered.

'That's right. She's right,' George Perry agreed. 'They had that place back of the Pococks. Snow up to the thatch, there were. Yes, I remember that, all right.'

'Poor lovers,' Mrs Beesley said. 'They found Miss Alice on the toilet, so I heard, and Jessica at the breakfast table. Boiled eggs untouched and the tea made.'

'Like Pompeii,' Wilf said.

'I thought they died in hospital,' Mr Beesley said, looking round enquiringly, and as if quite willing to be corrected.

Old Mr Combe's overcoat collar stirred. 'In nineteen forty,' he snarled, 'even the bloody rabbits starved. And –'

'In nineteen sixty-three,' Wilf started up, 'many wild creatures died. Our native birds flew south in flocks from the cold, and even those northern migratory birds, such as the fieldfare and redwing, were forced on further south. And in that year –'

'There weren't many birds in –'

'The Thames at Hampton Court in London froze over,' Wilf got in quickly.

'There weren't many birds in nineteen seventy-nine,' Jim Howel pressed on, 'flying south or anywhere else. And do you know for why? Eh?'

Jim folded his arms and waited.

Frowning, Wilf pushed the empty peanut bag round in a circle with a finger.

'Because,' Jim told him then, 'they were falling out of the sky. Their wings frozen. Solid as a Sunday boiler. That's why, boy!'

Stifling a smile he must have worn in the classroom while waiting for the question to get round to him, Wilf began, 'it's true that in certain coastal areas in the east, seagulls were found –'

Jim closed his eyes. 'Falling-out-of-the-bloody-sky-I'm-telling-you!'

'And milk bottles,' Mrs Beesley said.

Everybody looked at her. Her plump hands on her handbag disappeared as she leaned forward. 'I've just remembered. The year they took June Fitch off. We had milk bottles exploding on the doorsteps. With the cold. 'Tis a wonder there were nobody hurt.'

The door opened and Stan the landlord backed in, clutching an armful of logs. More drinks were ordered, and the talk grew taller. Images flickering in that small bar of strolling to South Wales and back on the frozen Channel, foxes stalking the High Street like wolves with hunger, and bonfires burning on the skating rivers. While outside, the damp and windy darkness blew against the windows, and the dogs stretched in front of the fire twitched and dreamed.

A DAY IN FEBRUARY

O N A TELEGRAPH WIRE above the scurrying High Street, a mistle thrush perched unsteadily in the rain and a wind that smelt of cabbages and mud, swinging and whistling with a sort of monotonous defiance, like a small boy who refuses to come down.

The rain was driven off the brow of the hill, down through the village to stride the valley on stilts of wind, the rooks in the horse chestnuts below blown and glistening, their nests lodged like footballs in the bare swaying tops of the trees. The wind tore the smoke from village chimneys and sent the postman in his orange waterproofs ballooning up the High Street, and the vicar, crossing the churchyard into a sudden furious struggle with his umbrella, wrestling the black wilful cloth through the lychgate, casting it out before him.

It bullied old Mr Snell, shoving him every couple of steps back up the hill he was struggling down to catch the town bus. It lifted the no-nonsense tweed skirt of Miss Holsworth, spinster, up and about with her dogs no matter what the weather, and rattled the corrugated iron gates of George Perry's coal yard, before running on to kick over the empty dustbins outside the schoolhouse, and send them bowling down the playground like skittles.

And then, as if whistled back to the sea, it turned suddenly, taking the rain with it, seen on its way by Major Pocock, Master of Foxhounds and Chairman of the Bench, clattering up the High Street on his hunter. And on a gable end a starling sang, a long thin dribble of sound blown on the last of the wind as the sun broke through, its sudden brilliance running across the roofs of the village, and sending the damp shadows of the pines along the valley road sparkling down the hillside.

More like spring now, than February, we told each other, the High Street busy with women with pushchairs and retired men with dogs on their way to the post office and shop.

The church clock struck nine, the high clear notes sprinkled over the village like a benediction, and anoraked and mittened, children pressed around the doors of the schoolhouse as children have done since the commemorative stone was tapped into place by the reforming hand of the squire's wife, and the laborious, reluctant squeaking of chalk on slate could be heard on the still morning of a Victorian summer.

The sun glittered from a water colour of a blue sky, the air above the horse chestnuts loud again with rooks, their cries even more tangled and strident in the confused thievery and bickering of nesting time. Powder from the hazel catkins by the stream blew in a breeze and the alder trees, that in summer shaded a bridge built by monks, were bruised with a purple flowering, and the yellow points of the primrose were a small bright find among the winter drabness.

And from the wood below the village, the first of the guns were heard as the shadows lengthened into the afternoon, a blackbird singing into them under a thumbprint of a moon. The outline of buildings cut into the twilight as lights began to dot the village, the wide arched windows of the schoolhouse framing on classroom walls the powder-paint pictures done with a large brush and a small hand, of matchstick people and puffing houses and dad with a cow, the Animals of Africa roaring and altogether fierce enough for bedtime.

As the village and the hills beyond softened into a cameo of black against the lilac sky, the last, distant dry cough of a gun was heard from the wood. All afternoon a percussion of death had beat at the air, as barrel after barrel was emptied into the flocks of woodpigeons wheeling above, each barrel seeking the direct hit needed to bring one down. The gunfire hammering even louder at dusk, when the sun burnt itself out behind the trees and the birds came blindly in to roost.

The guns were finally lowered, the burnt-rubber smell from the barrels smoking on the damp air, and bulging game bags and the debris of food and drink were thrown into the back of Landrovers and the boots of cars. And they turned for home, bouncing along the rutted and horseshoe-punched ride, leaving behind the spilt feathers of birds and red cartridge cases shining among wet dead leaves.

The light of the evening star fluttered above the valley, fluttered and then held, and the rapid call of a woodpecker reached out across the wood like a question. Followed as loud as dawn for a moment by an answering chorus from other birds, as the curtains in the village above them were drawn against the night, and the wind picked up from the sea again.

PORTRAIT OF AN INN

WITHIN SINGING DISTANCE of each other, the Pike inn stands near the church at the heart of the village, its sagging roofs stained a cider-gold with weather and patched with lichen.

It dates from the mid-17th century, and was thatched until losing it to a fire in the 1950s, a beacon in the lampless dark of the valley for the fire engine from a nearby market town, its bell charging the imperilled air from six, still miles away. The men, all part-timers, piling out in a tangle of shouted orders, hoses and ladders, eyes sternly raking the upstairs windows for young girls in negligees and distress.

As the men of the village stood alone with their thoughts, watching their pub burn, and the women made more tea, a group of small boys, among the first on the scene from the terrace of farm cottages in the High Street, waited with a proprietorial air for the walls, or at least the rafters, to collapse. But when they put it up they cut into the land for its stone, the walls, nearly three-feet deep, rammed with local cob and faced with solid chalk and flint, its timbers weathered oak and hammered there with iron. The walls, and the rafters, smoking damply on into first light, held.

It was built in 1661, a year after the late, deposed king's epitaph, Exit Tyrannus, was joyfully painted out in London, and the landlord hung out the sign of the Black Boy in honour of a young monarch restored from exile.

Sometime in the 1870s, after being bought by a maternal forbear of Stan's wife, Molly, who stands at the head of well over a hundred years of unbroken family tradition, it was left to the eldest daughter. She, in 1877, married a foreman woodman on the squire's estate, and in wifely deference renamed the pub the Woodman.

And then occurred a scandal which can still unsheathe female expressions of indignation in the family today. Barely, it seems, was the paint dry on the new sign, when the foreman, a dashing fellow with his best brown bowler worn at a fast angle and a curled moustache like a wink, ran off with the second cook from the Big House.

But if the spurned wife declined at all, she obviously did not do so for long. Within six months she had a new man, and the pub a new name – the one it bears today.

A man who staggered with half-drowned pride into the village one Sunday morning embracing the corpse of a local legend, a pike. A whale of a pike, weighting 27lbs and nearly four-foot long, brought up roaring and snapping from the depths in a small tidal wave of fury and erupting lily pads. He sold off nearly all his belongings to pay for its preserving and mounting, and when he came to her he laid it proudly on top of his remaining odds and ends on a carrier's cart, and wheeled it through the village like a dowry.

Today, that fish still dominates the back bar. There, stuffed and suspended in its glass cage, chainsaw teeth exposed in a death snarl, one unconquered, fierce fishy eye staring off in the direction of the dart board, it lays in wait forever in a small silent riverscape of artistically arranged weeds and stones. But studying it, and the simple words etched on worn brass beneath, giving its fighting weight and date of capture, men still turn thoughtful, its ferocity and the drenched, turbulent deed of that day reaching them across the years like ripples.

Stone-cool in summer, and warmed and scented with log fires in winter, the pub has three bars, the main one, the original centre of the house, a dim, blue-flagged room, moist with the casky smell of centuries, with beer and cider in wooden barrels behind the bar. Molly joins her husband there after six of an evening, dressing for it, a scented, luminous blonde with the power to take thirty years off a man. Under the heady influence of her eyes widening in admiring disbelief, stolid, middle-aged customers are reduced to breast-beating youths, turning accounts of prosaic tasks about the home or farm into dragons slain, and laying them with casual pride at her feet.

On weekends the pub lets its hair down. In the room laid out like a Welsh front parlour indicated to strangers as the lounge bar, and known to family and friends as the best room the knitwork antimacassars are removed from the piano top, under the black colonnaded Victorian wall clock which stopped in some long-forgotten year at twenty to four, and Stan addresses himself to the keys.

Golden Oldies and show tunes, rock and roll, and Walking Together Down An English Lane, and I'll Call You Sweetheart, and the Folks Next Door, the older women of the village sitting bright-eyed over their Saturday night mixes, handbags clutched on laps.

And then, as he does every Saturday, Mr Neville, a dispensing chemist with a shop in a nearby market town, who wears a clipped moustache and a regimental badge on his blazer like a reprimand to a backsliding world, listens frowningly to Stan's 'intro', and eyes boring into the opposite wall, launches himself sternly into a Harry Secombe number.

Finally, towards the close, Tom Hewitt is urged to sing. A working shepherd until well into his seventies, and nearly ninety now, with yellow-white hair sitting as light as smoke on his head, and a face burned still with weather. One hand gripping his pint like a hook, he sings in a sweet, wavering voice without accompaniment, tales of hard days and harvests, and dalliances with girls called Helen and Mary beneath summer elms, his eyes as he sings closed on a memory of a village England that was young still when he was.

The past is always here, a door constantly opening and closing on fragments of other lives, muffled and dimly told from other rooms. It tugs at the mind when footsteps sound in the quiet times above a low ceiling; it's there in the light spilling onto the cobbles of a yard that was made for horses; in flagstones damp with barrels; in the smell of logs burning on a winter's dusk, when the fowls in the back yard walk the stable loft ladder to roost; in sunlight slanting through a mullioned window and corners dim with stone.

And it's there in the people themselves. In a face split with glee as sudden and giving as a child's; in the random, unhurried talk in accents shaped by the land; in the clumsy, bursting celebrations; in the insularity, and fermenting, terrier-like squabbles and ancient animosities; in the local scandal breathed with relish, and gossip as old as Chaucer.

While around them, the land is ploughed and the corn sown and reaped again, and the

seasons turn and break timelessly on the hills above.

PASSAGE TO SPRING

SWEETENED BY A TOWER of Norman stone, the bells of Lent, carrying on their ancient sides the names of saints and merchants, squires and parsons, rhymes and prayers, rang out over the village, their peal of eight tumbling in an avalanche of iron down and across the valley, the land from hillside to hillside drowned and ringing.

The sap rose in the bud and creatures, cocooned and near death, stirred in their waxy sleep as the earth's pulse strengthened, and the first colours of spring cut into the land like small healing wounds. On banks the sweet violet grew, and periwinkle and ground ivy and the stars of blackthorn flowers in lanes slashed and spiked still with winter. And in the wood in the palm of the valley, where the gabbling of woodpeckers chased through the stripped treetops like squirrels, the primrose, the first rose, flowered, a promise of summer in the winter soil.

Taking the road down and out of the village, one saw below, in the grounds of what was once the big house, the constant movement of rooks above the horse chestnuts, fluttering and falling at dusk, breaking like clods of earth above the mating trees. And in the lanes that twist through the valley, a blackbird sang, the notes charged now with courtship, flung high above a fall of dawn rain.

Tender-heavy and dark against the pasture land, the ploughed fields waited for the harrow and the spring corn, and in meadows where later the cattle would lie and the lambs run by the side of the ewes, new grass glowed under a morning of pale sun, and rabbit scuts flashed in the hedgerows. And sweet eyes bright with lust, the hares met in twilight circles and jack tumbled jill or was sent on his way by her, boxed and ringing across the maddening, doe-scented fields.

In the evening, at lambing time, the ewes drifted to their favourite field places, and soon the air quivered with the clamour of birth, the ewes waiting their turn bleating and nosing at the first born of others, the lambs dropped wet and kicking into the sudden, unfocussed light of the world.

Those in need of a foster mother were wrapped in old coats and sweaters and housed in boxes, or in the bottom cool-ovens of farmhouse Rayburns and Agas. There, snug in the warmth and good-smelling darkness, they gazed out amiably when one opened the door, looking, with their glass-like eyes and thick curls of wool, pink-stained with birth, like presents hidden and waiting for little girls and Christmas morning.

There were more than the usual number in need of succour that season, their bawling running through the village for a while like hooligans, waiting for the milk taken from the ewes, warmed and fed to them in front rooms and kitchens. The post mistress took two in, bringing them in with her when she opened up, paying out pensions and stamping postal orders with them sunk in a bed of old cardigans and torn forms in triplicate in a cardboard box next to the radiator. And Stan, the landlord of the Pike, a pub already overrun with dogs in the bars, chickens in the back yard and cats in the outhouses, set one up in an empty Cola box by the large stone fireplace. A soot-black lamb, frolicking when it had found its feet like a fire-blackened imp, sharing the perks of beer and crisps with the house dogs, and bedding down with a couple of them at night in a corner of the ash-warmed hearth.

Even Miss Holsworth, village spinster of austere, weathered visage and rigid views, responded. Gaining for herself an instant and thoughtful audience in the post office, when she saw the two lambs sucking blindly at their milk behind the counter, and exclaimed in a voice made loud with a lifetime's condemnation, and shrilled then with a high, unsteady eagerness, that she, too, had one in the oven.

We were pressed into foster service ourselves, by a friend with a goat herd. The nanny was a virgin, and the billy, a black noisome brute, as shaggy as a winter bison and nearly as big, his yellow eyes salted with lust, had gone at her without preliminaries. She'd high-stepped away from the encounter, wide-eyed and snorting, and five months later from the result of it two kids, Anglo-Nubians, with the long, pendulous ears of the breed sticking out like the functionally secured tresses of boisterous schoolgirls. Their eyes, with that look of having been born with a secret which continues to amuse, holding our faces steadily at feeding time, growing milk bright as the cholesterol ebbed in the bottle, the tips of their tongues under the teats like small wet slices of smoked salmon.

With the charm of all new-born animals, they tried their first feet, staggering and constantly threatening to topple, their long, smooth-jointed stilts of legs new and perplexing equipment to them as they gazed down from their unsteady height with an abstracted air, as if wondering where they'd put the instruction manual.

Meanwhile, the bleating of the lambs out on the fields grew lustier, short quivering bursts splitting the damp air as they followed, stiff-legged, the milk and warmth of their mothers, or romped on fine days, kicking their heels at life.

While in the pines along the valley road, a song thrush perched higher and higher among the green, trying to catch and to hold the sun. The reaching, darting notes threading the twilight, singing into the lengthening dusk of the days.

FLIGHT OF THE SNOW CUCKOO

I N THE MONTH that sees the arrival of the cuckoo and the first, salad-green leaves of the year, it snowed. And as we stepped out into the bright confident days of the month, brilliant days that called with a memory of summer, it hit us with the sudden cold shock of a snowball in the back of the neck.

It fell at the very end of the day and out of sky without warning. With the church clock striking midnight bell on bell like disaster, it goose-feathered down the night, falling steadily on the farmlands and the dark sleeping village below, the solitary light of the telephone box in the High Street burning among the swirling flakes like a Christmas lantern.

All winter it had failed to get a grip and now, on an early morning in spring, it sat on the village as fat as a bully.

The sun rose on a garden world speckled with bird tracks, and brushed with the prowling bellies of cats, gifted with sudden arctic vision, while in the buried High Street, under roofs thatched with snow, the first footsteps in this new white world followed the milkman from door to door. And along the valley road, where the tall pines stung the chilled sunlit air, the morning deliveries for the shop and pub arrived like relief from a watching world, the brave red of the post van, pushing through the mail no matter what, shining in their wake, the sound of the horn on its approach as clear and triumphant as brass.

And the villagers, waking to find the enemy on the doorstep, put the kettle on, and armed with woolies and shovels went out to meet it.

While in his premises at the bottom of the hill that tips the village into the valley, George Perry, coal merchant, now that his busy time of the year was over, slumbered on, blowing perhaps, above the coal heaps and black dust, dreams as clean and as swift as fishes.

And then the swagged net curtains his wife insisted on twitched, and abruptly parted. And framed between the bunches of lace like the thighs of a Victorian chorus girl, George's meaty features, topped with a begrimed and buckled cord cap, put on first thing, pressed against the panes. Only minutes later, army surplus boots hammered on the stairs, and George, a man with the bowed strength of a figure in an old Guinness advertisement, half emptied his yard onto the back of the lorry, and with a rescuing rush of corrugated iron gates, chugged, exhaust coughing and blowing, up into the village, eyes peeled for survivors and a sudden demand for coal.

And outside the school, when hostilities broke out, the air wet and wailing, and loud with the barking of dogs, snatch squads of young mothers braved the cross-fire of snowballs to dive into the rioting ranks, dragging their charges behind them through the gates, and into the custody of school.

Only Miss Holsworth, indomitable spinster of this parish, green-wellington booted and buttoned up in a shooting jacket like a stiff, awkward embrace, refused to make a fuss. Ash walking stick at the ready, should lust or impertinence rear, her two grey English Setters shambling like seals behind her in the snow, she made her way to collect her copy of The Times from the shop, as she would through fire, flood or invasion, her voice, when invited to remark on the sudden weather, brief and briskly bright, as if dealing with the rude remark of a child, made for effect and therefore best ignored.

Inside the post office, melted snow puddled the floor, and around a transistor radio on the counter tuned in for the weather forecast, a small group of villagers had collected, waiting, perhaps, for London Calling and the voice of Churchill and no surrender.

But we were not to be tested further. There was no more snow. And with the last of it glittering along the hills like salt, days of strengthening sun flushed what was left from the land and sent it running through the roadside springs, the air clean-breathed and scented again with the frail brilliances of the earth, the church bells of Easter breaking over the village like a spring shower.

BILL SIKES

THE LAST MORNING of his life was one of sudden flawless beauty; a glittering warmed jewel of a morning, given to him as if a gift.

He was a large, pure-white boxer dog, six stone of packed fluent muscle, pulling ahead of the two boxer bitches as usual on that morning. A dog of a dog, full of his prime, strutting it out, centre of the road like an invitation or a challenge.

We'd had over a week of grey skies and rain and as we took the road out of the village on that drab dawn in early May, the fields were lost in a ground mist and the wood below held the weather like a marsh.

And then, in the lanes beyond the wood, with only a gradual, almost imperceptible, flush of warmth and light to tell of its coming, the sun gathered and rose above the brow of a hill. Rose burning in a dissolving mist, the valley steaming beneath it, the air as we walked shining like a thing newly and frailly grown.

The climbing sun struck sparks from the fields of dew, the air above them rushed with lark song, and the dogs, freed from their leads, chased after this new bright world like a thrown ball.

Heads down after the scents of the morning, bloodhound-like in ditches and along banks, their scuts of tails an ecstatic blur, they quartered the lanes in a burst of energy as uncomplicated as a shout.

And Sikes, wearing a black eye of dirt from a rabbit burrow, and ditch mud on his legs like disreputable socks clean on that morning, careless under the sudden beneficence of the day, heedless of how or why. A Just William of a dog with the sun and the high road calling, trotting ahead with that sideways rolling gait of his to meet them.

He arrived at the age of six weeks in a shopping basket carried by my wife at a time when we were between dogs, and entered our world in a small explosion of savaged book covers, chewed furniture and missing, presumed buried, shoes. We christened him Bill Sikes because his Toby-jug villainous looks seemed to carry that name already, like an inscription stamped on his bottom.

But despite what it said on the outside, his was essentially a mild disposition; a disposition that was quite prepared to allow humankind and the rest of the dog world their space, if they would allow him his. Although he would never remember a previous engagement when it came to a fight, he would never start one, and dogs intent that he should involve himself in the sport soon emerged from it wishing they had left well alone. Sikes, with the agility of the breed and the business end of his six stone, would finish it before it had a chance to get started by flipping them over on their backs, and then growling meditatively while holding them there, as if wondering which bit to chew on first.

But they always escaped unchewed. Sikes being pulled off or trotting away, confident and quite content in leaving behind a lesson well taught.

With old people and small animals, he was either indifferent or, if he decided to involve them in his world, mindful of his power and fanged strength. He once, presumably for the sheer hell of it, chased and caught a rabbit. Scooping it up without breaking stride, he went the full circle of a three-acre field as triumphant as a greyhound who has finally got the hare.

And when he did trot back to us, we steeled ourselves for bloodied fur and whimperings of pain. But as Sikes opened his jaws, the rabbit, damp and bit chewed looking, and no doubt a little confused, dropped to the ground in one piece, and reorienting itself, took off, ears flattened, for the nearest hedge.

With children he was as patient as a seaside donkey, and with adults friendly but aloof under the admiring word or hand. It was for us, the people who fed and walked him, that he reserved the works. To wrestle him off a chair or, simply so we could get in it, the bed, was to unleash a rising, bloodcurdling chorus of snarls and growls, spittle bubbling like a lubricant for those terrible, bared teeth.

But there was of course no harm in it. Not in Bill Sikes, with his battered bowler and red-spotted kerchief tied at the throat, growling stage curses from that Dickensian underworld where all shadows are larger than life.

And it was, I suspect, those shadows, thrown against a backdrop of memory that was at the heart of so much of the affection given to him in this life. Sikes was a dog who seemed to appeal to men more than women, and I believe that it was an appeal which went back to childhood and innocence. He belonged in that cupboard in the imagination of a man where the wooden swords, catapults and bent pins for fish hooks are stashed still. He was tramp, pirate, outlaw and Dick of the Bloody Hand in the day-dreaming underworld of the small boy. A half-remembered figure that beckoned outside a classroom window when the sun shone and the lessons droned, to follow, carelessly and gloriously free, Sikes on some country road forever summer.

It was, we were told, his heart. That muscle which had given him so much boisterous life suddenly failed him.

We returned from the walk that morning with the sun still climbing, Sikes strutting ahead of us, swaggering through the gate as if bringing it home, a shower of bright coin over his shoulder. When he faltered, faltered and then fell.

He tried to rise, his face a terrible and deeper shade of white, distress and bewilderment in his eyes. And the knowledge, finally, that whatever had struck at him with such dreadful force was not to be flipped over on its back this time; was not something he could trot away from, confident and content in leaving behind a lesson well taught.

He died some minutes after we reached the vets' practice. Reviving in the car on the way there, he shouldered his way through the door of the surgery, Sikes again, centre of the road and ready for anything, out on his own with us as he was in the beginning. The hand that had struck him down, and held him there for the first time in the five, game years of his life, forgotten.

In the reception, he jumped up and put two paws on the counter. A dog sure of his welcome, and poised there still in my memory, Bill Sikes, breasting the bar of the Pickwick Arms. Before falling back as if pushed, and lying there, still, on his side.

Rushed onto the surgery table, surrounded by humans in a drama of attempted resuscitation, he died as he had lived. In a circle of attention, centre of the road, upstaging us to the end.

VILLAGE WEDDING

W E STOOD along the lane or leaned against the warmed mossed stone of the churchyard wall, the air drowsy and stroked with the scent of lilac, and told each other again that it couldn't be a more perfect day for them. A gilded summer's day, sparking with butterflies, bees sinking among the pollen in village gardens and the fields of clover, and cuckoos calling across the mowing grass.

Children ran among us in small riots, the men talking among themselves, the women sharing their laughter like secrets. A father shifted the weight of his daughter on his shoulders, and the horsewoman who'd paused on her morning trot through the village turned, saddle creaking, to check she was causing no obstruction, the great bay tossing his head impatiently, bridle jingling like coin in the sudden silence.

The two photographers who'd been lounging under the young green of the lime trees, had moved to the church doors, and ahhh, the women breathed, and dreamed with their eyes, putting aside for that moment what is, or was, or might be, and allowing only what should be. Oyster-grey satin and a veil lifting in a June breeze, and the church bells ringing the changes, spilling in a fall of silver across the valley as the young couple stepped out of the ancient dimness, into sunlight and a shower of confetti and rice.

Starched, pressed and pinned with flowers, the men of the wedding party gathered one side of the church doors, the women the other, the lowered eyes of the bridesmaids scything through the watching crowd, bringing down the local youths in giggles and sudden confusion. And then the photographs, framed moments for the family album and the tops of mantelpieces and sideboards, and the gaze of future generations.

'There she is, that's Sharon there ...'

'But she was beautiful!'

'Took her hours to get that hat on right ...'

'That's great Uncle Jason at the back there, isn't it?'

'Yes. He made one of the speeches afterwards, at the reception. '

'Doesn't he look young!'

'I can hear 'ee now ...'

'Look at those clothes! How funny!'

The first photographer glanced up from his camera. 'Can we see more of the ladies, please?' he asked.

'As much as they want to show, eh, lads?' the second photographer said, backing artistically away among the gravestones, among past generations of the same families, and winking at the males shoulder to shoulder in a scrum of grim awkwardness.

The bride's mother, creaking with corsetry and authority, went among the ranks like a sheepdog, breaking up the men and herding in the women, thrusting them, with their colours and frills and the froth of hats, like flowers into the embarrassed hands of the males.

And then the bride and groom. She flushed and shining with the day, moving the veil from her face like hair, he full of shyness one moment, shouldering pride the next. The bloom of a scrubbed hangover from last night's stag party on his broad face, grinning at his mates, winking and pulling faces at them in the manner of a member of the audience dragged up to assist in one of the acts.

The oak lychgate of the church had been tied shut with rope, a local custom of great age dating to the untying of knots by the groom on the gown of his bride. And this groom, stepping ahead of his bride, squared up to them, his beefy hands getting to grips with it as if it were some obscure test of manhood.

Blushing and serious browed, he ignored the laughter and comments: 'Just pretend you'm trying to get into the Pike, John, afore last orders.'

And to his bride: 'You go ahead and wait at the hotel, m'dear. We'll send 'ee on when 'ee's finished.'

He untied the last knot, and in relief and confusion resorted to strength, swooping up his bride and carrying her like plunder off to the waiting car.

The white hired Rolls, streaming with ribbons, the polish on it catching the sun like snow, did a triumphant tour of the village, and passing the church again pulled up at the Pike some yards further on where Stan and Molly were waiting at the door to greet them. Molly dressed as if for Saturday night, Stan in a suit, cricket tie ironed to a gloss, their two teenage daughters rushing from bride to bridesmaids and back again, gasping and squealing with delight at the sudden flood of satin and lace.

The cake was cut and the best man stood up to speak. 'I've known John a tidy few years now, even since in fact we wur at primary school together here in the village ...'

And John, sitting with his bride at the head of the table, hung his head as if listening to a particularly convincing closing speech for the prosecution.

Iced bottles of champagne bristled from

large improvised wooden flower tubs, among food piled as thick as a jumble sale on trestle tables borrowed from the village hall. Draped with impeccable linen, they shouldered slabs of cheese, meat pies, pickled onions, pates, dips, quiches and salad bowls, baked pink hams, cold meats, cottages loaves, pickled walnuts, boiled eggs and sausage rolls.

Champagne corks went off like fireworks, showering pink health on the young couple, the raised glasses around the room brimming with good wishes.

Knifes were sharpened, and wedges of this and slabs of that and piles of the other were loaded onto plates, with only lettuce and a slice of ham for Jim's wife because she was on a diet, and no pickled onions for Uncle Nat because of his teeth – and glasses of sherry, gin, whisky, rum, port-and-lemon, ale, wine, lager and cider-punch were lifted and clinked, and filled again.

The vicar looked in, circulated brightly, kissed the bride and, mistaking him for the groom, shook with vigorous sincerity the hand of the bemused best man, and with a few rambling directions to guide him along his marital journey, finished his sherry and left.

The knitwork antimacassars were removed from the piano top, and Stan, loosening his tie, settled determinedly at the keys.

A new barrel of the local cider, Five Jacks, its name stencilled on it like a warning, was tapped. The best man got up on a chair, fired into another speech, which not even he seemed to understand, a bridesmaid was sick, politely, into an ashtray, and two of the men had to be restrained from taking their coats off to each other. And Mr Neville the dispensing chemist was seen in the honeysuckle hedge in the back yard, locked in a damp and desperate embrace with Miss Prout, schoolmistress and occasional church organist. And throughout it all, like a Greek chorus telling of misery in the uproar, someone's maiden aunt wept steadily in a corner and refused to be consoled.

And then it was time for the bride and groom to leave for their honeymoon. But the groom could not be found.

The house and backyard and outhouses were searched, including the old stable loft where, on Sunday mornings, the odd Saturday night drunk has been found as warm as an egg in the straw kept there for the nesting boxes, but no bridegroom, sleeping or otherwise engaged, was to be found.

The bride's mother confronted the groom's mother, and the groom's mother, in tones of having pulled a fast one, told the bride's mother, the bride, and the room at large that her son was now somebody else's responsibility. And dumping herself down on a chair, handbag clutched firmly on lap, folded her mouth obstinately.

And then one of the bride's more distance relatives, who, on arriving at the reception, had parked her husband down, allowed him a small, drowned whisky, and herself a small sherry, and had sat throughout with the expression of someone taking a last and deeply hypocritical look at the deceased, had her say. 'Never did have much sense, that family,' she sniffed loudly. 'Fancy running off after you've got married.'

And the bride, as she was meant to, heard it. Standing alone, a bride without her groom, the tears that had been trembling on the brink throughout her day finally fell, silencing the room in their abandonment. Her bridesmaids, with squeals of concern, and spitting looks of fury at the offending relative, rushed to her side and wrapped her in a comforting damp bandage of satin.

While the two families took sides and the insults started to fly, the groom, standing diffidently in the doorway, went unnoticed for some moments. Pale faced, and with the crust of cowpats on his knees from the field behind the pub, where he had purged himself of the day's excesses, he coughed politely to draw attention to his presence, and smiled wanly into the room.

Holding his bride, who had fallen, sobbing even more violently on his shoulder, he looked with reddened eyes at his guests on the verge of battle, at the debris of food and drink, and at the aunt, still weeping steadily in the corner, and said quietly, and to no one in particular, 'Tis the champagne that does for I.'

A TRIP TO THE SEASIDE

WE ROSE EARLY one morning in summer, a spruce and shiny morning, prinked and polished with dew. And leaving the still-sleeping village behind, breasted the hill in a burst of brass from the sun, and turned towards that glimpse of the sea which could be seen between a gap in the hills of the valley, calling on hot summer days like the music of a carnival heard only streets away.

On we strode, under showers of dawn birdsong, splashing through deep-banked lanes where the sun fell in pools, a blackbird, caught napping, stuttering alarm in flight as we passed beneath it, in stern and purposeful silence, on towards the sea.

Stopping only to point with military fingers at the Ordnance Survey map, or to take with an air of half-rations a sandwich and flask-top of tea, we left the farms behind where dogs had barked and the cocks crowed as if the sun were marching past. Through hamlets and villages, arriving with the milk and the post, and out the other side, the sea running head of us, peeking and then gone again, between the moving hills.

Until filling our lungs with the shell-pink smell of it, we paused on the top of the hill which runs down into the town like a play slide.

The tide out, the sea waited at the end of the beach. 'There it is,' we told each other, and rolled the air round our mouths judiciously.

Below us, the sand and deserted sea front sprawled like toys put aside at bedtime. The jumbled roofs of the town steamed through the morning haze, seagulls gliding and calling above them, and in the bedrooms of hotels and guesthouses holidaymakers drifted with the sun and sea in their dreams, buckets and spades and buoyant rubber waiting for their sleepless children like Christmas morning.

We walked down into the blue and white painted town, along early morning pavements swept and waiting, the shop blinds rolled like coloured sticks of rock, the cast on the violently cheerful posters for The Summer Show For All The Family dying on the empty streets like a club comic.

Along the front, the gulls whining and plucking at the air, a youth doused the pavement outside an amusement arcade and beat at it with a bass broom. And on the beach a solitary figure of an old woman, wearing what appeared to be a dressing gown tied at the waist with a bow of blue string, held a cluster of carrier bags in one hand, and with the other prodded irritably at the sand with a walking stick, as if to wake it up.

The smell of breakfast followed us as the sun climbed, the tinkle of the tea things from hotels and boarding houses running along the front like a genteel breeze. And in a lull of dreaming, empty sea and sand, images flickered in the memory like a What the Butler Saw machine. Pictures once seen of a Victorian beach with enveloping costumes that never touched water, and unsinkable hats in case, perhaps, they should. Of home movies showing some girl with bobbed hair running, laughing, down to the sea, and then, without turning, running back again, forward and back again, to the wound-up tune of the Charleston in some suburban front parlour. And paper hats and Kiss Me Quick, and arm-in-arm along a postwar front when the lights came on again.

And then the sea shook itself, and turned towards the town. And we made our way down to the harbour to see what boats the tide would bring in.

We walked along the cobbled quayside, wrapped in blue sea breezes like silk, the sun racing towards us, skimming across the water. Here and there a few scattered figures waited, the old men among them, home for good from the sea, weathered almost to wood, burned and aged to a single, unsayable thought as they gazed steadily at the horizon, the tide moving beneath them.

The boats came in on the flood, the thrown ropes caught and anchored, men, scaly with fish, climbing the quayside ladders as mysterious to us as divers. And then suddenly, as if blown across there from the high street, women with shopping bags were everywhere. Drawn like seagulls to the fish laid out on the cobbles, falling on the catches as they were priced, prodding and peering, some of them, landladies perhaps, holding up mackerel by the tails with an expression of something left behind between the sheets.

The horizon of the sea rose glittering with the sun, and broke over the town in a shower of light. And like a weather-clock, the doors of hotels and guesthouses opened, and holidaymakers set off for the beach as if for work in a rush hour of bucket and spades, towels, sun hats, paperbacks and oil, their children hugging armfuls of inflated dinghies, seahorses and water wings that couldn't wait, or were dressed already for the deep, small boys in goggles and snorkels, periscoping down the high street.

The blinds closed over the shops as the sun gathered and struck at the town, the streets snarling with traffic. Goods vehicles and family cars, and cars with surf boards on top nosing among them like sharks, bikers in leathers and racing cyclists with caps on back to front, caravaners and day-tripping charabances, the faces gaping behind the great bowls of glass like goldfish.

On the front, women with laughs like candyfloss and men with red braces jostled past men in orange pants and sea-going plimsolls, for gripping, after lunch, the pitching cobbles outside the Admiral Coddington or Lord Nelson, and chubby-naked infants with moustaches of ice-cream darted under trays of tea, crisps, hot-dogs, Coke, hamburgers and sandwiches, borne down onto the sands.

The crowded sea was churned white with activity, children climbing and jumping all over it like some large amiable pet. And the morning stirred and slid lazily into the afternoon in a heat haze of cooking flesh and sand, bodies turning and browned in oil, or plunging, as red as lobsters, into the boiling sea.

We took a last walk along the front, where seagulls loitered like touts outside the food kiosks and the air smelt of hot-dog onions and chips, the sound of Space Invaders from the arcades ricocheting around us. And on the strolling promenade, families and young couples went by while the old sat in deckchairs, or nodded there, old ladies in their summer dresses drowsing as if held in an embrace, stroked by memories and the sun.

And we paused again on the hill above the seaside town, and looked back at its silent, shrieking and splashing distance. The cliffs and crisp blue sky as remotely golden and impossible now as those that called from long-ago railway posters of childhood and endless summer.

WASSAILING AND THINGS

THE DAY had been dizzy with heat, a midsummer's day brought bellowing to its knees in fields where the cattle lay prostrate and the lee of walls were littered with sheep. And now, sun-sapped and taunted by a cuckoo beating its way across the back of the pub, we stood in the murmuring dimness of the Pike, the cider running from the tap as clear and as green as shallows.

The vicar, a truant figure in pressed jeans and an open-necked shirt of the sort of blue check that sighs for boyhood, lowered his dutiful pint of Five Jacks. 'Where was I?' he asked.

'Something about that book you wur reading, Vicar,' George Perry supplied. 'Wassailing and things.'

'Of course. Thank you, George.' The vicar's smile fell on George like a halo.

Pleased and embarrassed, George squared his shoulders, his chest, after an afternoon spent in a deckchair in his coal yard, rearing out of his shirt and khaki braces like an inflamed bull's.

Jim Down looked at him with interest. 'What's that then, George? Wassailing?'

'Search I,' George said with a touch of astringency. Jim Down, a forester, had a growing sideline in fire logs.

'Is it dancing round the cider tree and that, Vicar?' Wilf Perkin, who'd been to grammar school, asked brightly.

The vicar beamed down at him from his pale height of six-foot three. 'Something of that sort, Wilf, yes,' he said, as if sharing a joke. 'But terribly interesting, I thought,' he added, and raised his glass with an air of conclusion.

A conscientious man, the vicar had applied himself assiduously to the living since arriving a few months before, each tentative approach made to the community like an exploring hand around a female waist.

'An old custom,' George Perry said, filling the conversational gap.

'Ancient,' Wilf said more specifically.

'Bound to be,' Jim Down chipped in, and indicated to Stan the landlord that he wanted to buy a round. Stepping over one of the pub dogs simmering noisily on the cool stone of the floor, Stan bent to the cider barrel.

'Yes, it goes back apparently,' the vicar said with the timing of a salesman, 'to the fifth century.'

Wilf nodded slowly, as if to say that he would have put it about there himself.

'Like a lot of these ancient customs independent of the church,' the vicar went on, 'it's a propitiatory practice, of course. Appeasing the spirits of the fields and trees, et cetera.'

The syllables of 'et cetera' came out like a schoolmasterly rap across the knuckles. Then he smiled down at them, equals in enlightenment. 'But harmless enough,' he added, almost mouthing the words, as if not wishing to spoil the fun.

'It's roots –' He blinked with surprise at the fresh pint Stan had put in front of him, and with a flustered air finished the remains of his old one.

'It's roots of course go deep into history. Deep.' The vicar paused and his eyebrows lifted. 'Rather good that, I thought. Roots, cider-tree...'

He laughed, a sudden high sound like a shout. And one hand gliding in like a large speckled fish, delicately parted both sides of his shirt collar from his neck, and frowned at the ceiling as if seeking a source of irritation.

'No, it occurred to me,' he pressed on, 'that I – that's to say, the village – those interested might reinstate, as it were, some of those old customs...Well, wassailing for example.'

A few more customers drifted in through the open door, their figures turned to shadows for a moment against the parched light outside. Stan put down the copy of the local paper he was reading.

George looked up doubtfully at the vicar. 'What, dancing round a tree and all that, Vicar?'

'There was no dancing involved, George,'

the vicar said, sounding tired. 'Simply a cup, cider cup, filled with wine – that's to say, apple-wine, cider. Then –'

'Laced with gin, Vicar,' Stan put in.

He was checking one of the pints, holding it up to the naked bulb that burned in the bar day and night, the cider gleaming now a pale milky-gold under it. The vicar stared at the draught with starched blue eyes.

'Laced with gin, Stan?' Wilf Perkin said, and frowned, as if considering an unlikely chemical formula.

'Oh, yes. I remembered they at it. Buggers they wur.' Stan smiled an apology at the vicar and bent to the barrel again. 'Then there was faggot burning.'

'Around the cider-tree?' The vicar's head went back as if singed by the image.

'Noa. Different custom altogether, Vicar,' Stan said kindly.

The sun was going down now, spinning down a wheat-coloured sky, burning itself out against the deep and ancient windows of the pub, the air oiled with the evening scent of honeysuckle from the hedge of it in the back yard.

Stan finished with the round and tossed the money into the cash drawer. 'They used to drink a pint of cider to each strip of wood binding the faggots, see. Well, could amount to fifteen pints or more sometimes.'

'All with a drop of gin in them?' George Perry looked impressed.

'Noa, George, that wur wassailing,' Stan said, the words falling like clotted cream. 'No, with the faggots they'd toast them, like, then throw 'em on the fire there.'

'Themselves as well, along with 'em, I shouldn't wonder. Fifteen pints of Five Jacks!' John Down said, and winced.

The first of the haymakers piled in with their thirsts, spokes of light from the dying sun wheeling in after them, oil stains and the dust of hay on brown skins, their hair tangled and snarled with sweat.

Stan set a handful of empty pint pots up on the counter, the glasses polished with light in the gloom.

'But what about the actual ceremonies, Stan?' the vicar asked plaintively, and as if Stan were much further away. The vicar's features had taken on a flushed and brittle animation.

'Well, it wur'nt the ceremonies as such, Vicar,' Stan said. 'I don't remember much of they. No, 'twere more like – well, the atmosphere, I suppose...'

The vicar stared almost wildly at Stan's back stooped over the cider barrel. And then at the glass in his hand, as if seeking an answer there, and lifting it to his mouth found it empty.

More of the field workers crowded in and a move was made to sit down, George with a proprietorial air escorting the vicar to one of the settles next to the fireplace, where the faggots had roared and the wassailing parties had stood with ritual and the iron smell of a January night on them. Filled now, in midsummer, with a large urn of foxgloves, honeysuckle and bracken.

From the press of bodies in the bar, the air crackled with energy. An energy which seemed to spark between the men like static, raw with the smell of the fields and fruitfulness.

And the vicar, with another empty glass in front of him, and his head resting on the high back of the settle, watched the shadows moving on the whitewashed walls of the pub like the reflection of flames, his eyes as gently amused now as a child's.

SUMMER'S END

THE GREEN of the wheat fields deepened, turning to gold, fired with a pale brittle flame as the valley burned with summer. Burned in a heatwave of simmering mornings and charred dusks, when field poppies flared in the twilights and the nights held the heat of the day like a cooling stone.

Under skies bleached by the sun, the valley dozed and droned through the days, days of bumble bees and dragonflies and adders. The lanes were clotted with summer, its scents clinging as thick and as warm as wool to hedges of honeysuckle, dog rose and blackberry, the bank grasses seared with the heat, the husks of cow parsley falling to rust.

Walking down from the hills, the baked air crackling and jumping with insects, one followed the road down the valley side to the village, down in a ramshackle fall of stone, slate and thatch, to where swallows murmured in the eaves and it was summer in the High Street. The sound of radios playing on bikinied lawns, deckchairs, and pop and ice-cream from the shop, and Panama hats stalking with English coolness the scented jungles of hollyhocks and sunflower, the heated colours of front gardens bruising the eye.

Church bazaars and village fetes, and long, murmuring Sunday afternoons, when the starched crackle of applause could be heard from above the village, where the green, yellow and white pavilion, repainted for the season and varnished now by the sun, sat on the cricket field like a beached Victorian pleasure boat. White flannels against the green, running up to bowl, the chop of leather on oiled yellow, and across the valley the breaking voice of a cuckoo calling. The spectators sitting in deckchairs in front of the pavilion, or sprawled under the beeches lining the field, the shadows of the great trees lengthening as the midges swarmed, and twenty were needed for victory and five wickets still to fall.

The fields of corn, darkened by August suns to saffron, were harvested just in time, and the weather broke finally in a night storm. The glazed air split with it, the valley deep, green mysterious water under the sudden brilliances of light.

And up on the valley road a mistle thrush, shaken into song by the brief unholy daylight and thunderous dark, sang out as the storm rolled out to sea. The notes sounding clear across the singed and waiting silence, as the first drops broke on the yellowing leaves and the parched earth below.

SEASON OF MISTS AND
BRONCHITIC CHURCH MICE

T HE SWIFTS that had rushed the
village skies at dusk, screaming like
an ambush, swooping the length of
the High Street, ringing the church tower and
back again, had mostly gone now. And the
wheat was cut and the straw baled under trees
stained with the first colours of autumn, and
the marauding smoke of stubble fires drifted
across fields.

And we woke to September, and spiders'
webs glittering on hedgerows and rough
pasture, the air above the valley tarnished with
the first mists of the season, lingering on into
mornings of muffled sunlight, field mushrooms
and dew.

Harvest fattened the barns of the valley,
and in his study in the eighteenth-century

vicarage, where the bronchitic mouse wheezed and sang behind the wainscot, the vicar sat over his sermon of thanksgiving as the churchyard limes began to turn. The church above the reaped fields shining with the praise of a roster of village woman, the starched altar linen burning in stained-glass twilights, ready to receive the gifts of the year.

And on still nights, the flight call of redwings could be heard again, wintering flocks of them moving across the valley, and swallows and martins and the last of the swifts barbed the telegraph wires above the High Street, waiting to depart.

And in his coal yard at the bottom of the hill, George Perry took delivery of the first tipper loads of winter stock, watched by the usual audience of small boys. George, shovel in hand, prowling the growing heaps of coal and coke, on the lookout in the noise and dust for buried boys and short measure.

The church was decorated with corn, its barn-like silence lifted with the voices of children singing. The tins of food they'd brought to school, to be distributed afterwards to the old of the village, piled gifts stacked around the altar, with offerings from village gardens, and allotments and kitchens, and the gift of bread.

The trees turned, the bronze of the sheltering field hedge oaks, nailed and armoured against all the weathers of the valley, to rust, the wood below the village to russet and brown, copper, red and gold. And summer was an old lion now, going down, the wounds of autumn in his side.

The horse chestnuts in the grounds of what was once the squire's house grew ragged with decay, the great domes a splendour in their ruin, their summer shades holed now and letting in the weather. The spiked fallen fruit, plundered by squirrels, and generations of village boys for that one conker which, threaded with string and armoured in vinegar, would raise them to glory, split and gleaming among the gathering leaves.

The valley burned and crackled with autumn, rich with the bounty from its trees and brambled lanes of berries, and the rotting windfalls in orchards, the elder bushes hung with feeding blackbirds and starlings, and sparrows fluttering for insects on hedges of flowering ivy, and jays on the acorns. And other worlds among the hedgerows and growing litter of leaves, hedgehog nests and wintering beetles and caterpillars, and toads snug in mouse holes, scurrying bank voles and the chattering of harvest mice, and the pin-fight squeals of shrews.

And in the wood below the village, where a lone robin sang, sweet, sad needles of song falling, food was gathered and buried, and a badger sniffed the air, and bottom-first dragged more bedding into its sett, making it up for winter. While above us on the hills of the valley, the first calves of the season butted at the milk of their mothers, and tractors, flying their lines of starlings and gulls, crawled soundlessly, harrowing the burnt stubble for the winter ploughing, the autumn flocks of lapwings gathering over the turned earth.

There were days of rain and winds from the sea, the blown fluffy fruit of rosebay willowherb and wings of sycamore scattered on them. And still, clear days smelling of autumn, the air sharp with a memory of winter and sweetened with decay. Days when no leaves seemed to fall nor animal stir, a kestrel, hunting the slopes of the valley, hanging endlessly in the sky, the mornings harsh with rooks above the horse chestnuts, their damp-throated cries drifting up through the village.

And the post mistress, after the first frost warning, put out more water and extra fat and nuts for the birds. And lagging them with bits of old carpet and bracken from the lanes, tucked her fig trees up for winter.

Fog and rain, and the rot of more frosts, and autumn ran now like a damp fire through the valley, leaves withering and falling before it. Drifts of them shining in morning mists along the roadsides, kicked and scuffed through by children on their reluctant way to school.

And days when the sun shone, a whisky-gold light falling on the wasted woodland, smoking like wreckage in the still, ruined silences. Days that sent the village men out armed with spades into gardens and allotments to break the soil for manure and the spring sowing, and fires burned in dusks when robins sang and the smoke of leaves scented the air.

The windows of the post office and shop bristled now with fireworks, boxes of sparklers and bangers, Catherine wheels, skyrockets and shower-bombs, fat with the gaudy explosive promise of bonfire night, and gangs of children plundered for firewood and totted at village doors for clothes for the guy.

The lights burned in the village hall for rehearsals of the pantomime, the home-made wine and photography competitions, the slimming, craft, dance and table tennis clubs, the keep-fit classes and WI lectures on dried-flower arranging, baking and jam-making, and new things to do with apples. The nights frost bright and shining with autumn under slender translucent moons. The skies above the valley piping with the movement of more flocks from the north, and the clamour of wild geese carrying winter on their wings.

A CHRISTMAS STORY

H E HAD MADE the round-topped table under the front window from beechwood. At its centre, rooks flew over a stand of winter elms, and in a broad belt around the edge of it a carousel of small animals ran and tumbled in demented, secret delight.

Nathaniel touched each animal in turn, and as if for the first time, named them: Rabbit, Stoat, Hare, Shrew, Mole, Squirrel, Rat, Otter, Fox and Badger.

On top of the television and a sideboard, and hung on the walls, were displayed some of his other wood carvings. Among them a Romany vardo, with a couple of tethered ponies cropping the verge; a retriever with a plump pheasant in its mouth; a team of two Shire horses, the drag and weight of the plough cut into their shoulders; and a vixen, head up to the wind, her mask tight with concentration and need.

And on a round wall plaque, a small bird encircled by thorns. The bird, Nathaniel told me, was a robin, the thorns those of the hawthorn, from which was made the Crown of Christ.

The breast of the robin, Nathaniel said with an edge of impatience, as if he'd had to explain this many times before, was, in the beginning, white. But it went to our Lord bleeding on the cross, holding water for Him in its beak. And came away from Him with His blood on its face and on its breast. Which is why the robin is said to be so confiding in man, and why its winter song sounds of lament.

We sat down by the fire and refilled our glasses.

We were drinking cider laced with gin because it was Christmas Eve. In the small tiled fireplace ash logs burned steadily, helped along by Nathaniel who gave them a poke now and then with his stick, sweetening the air with their scent.

There was a refugee air about the old man, sitting with his wood carvings in that neat and otherwise featureless room. A man who had left the rest of his past behind, who had been fed and numbered and was waiting now only for some sort of collection.

We were sitting in the front room of his old people's bungalow, one of a cul-de-sac of them tucked away in a corner of the council estate on the edge of the village, their oblong windows giving them a vacant look, the small clipped lawns in front like bibs for mouths.

Nathaniel was nearly ninety, a big man, his physical decline sitting on him like an ill-fitting suit. Over half a century in the fields had weathered his body, his muscles hard with knots which pained and held him stiff.

In a worn leather-framed photograph on the mantelpiece, a young Nathaniel posed with his new wife outside a terraced cottage, their first home together, one arm hugging her to him, and looking straight into the camera with a smile as confident as a wink. His wife, Flora, had the look of a woman pulled laughing in protest from the kitchen, taking off her apron perhaps and tidying herself as she went, and half resisting now, as if in the sudden company of strangers, the teasing arm around her, composing herself for the serious business of having your photograph taken.

'We were married near sixty years, me and Flora. Sixty years along o' me. She's dead now. Yes ...'

He reached for his tobacco tin and papers on the mantelpiece, the edges of the tin showing through silver, a scratched and faded picture of a bearded Tar of the King's Navy on the lid.

'She were a good mate to I, my Flora. My mommet. We had some good times together. And some bad, mind. Ohh, yes. And some bad.'

Nathaniel teased a thin line of tobacco along the cigarette paper, his movements slow and a little shaky, his large, blue-veined hand knotted and stained with age, the little finger bent with an old break. The result, he'd told me earlier, of a fight with Big Willie Boswell, a travelling man up for the apples. They'd followed the Romany rule, stripped to the waist on a fighting mark made that day nearly sixty years ago by the heel of a boot in the grass behind one of the cider orchards. A mark to which the loser, Big Willie Boswell, afterwards failed to come up to.

'A girt big bastard, 'ee were. Used to wear a woman's scarf round his neck, and a gold pin, a horseshoe, near as big as a pony's. Rings on his fingers. His brother, Nelson, told him to take 'em off first. I can see 'ee now, Willie. Built like a Shire, prison tattoos up his arms, standing there. I got a hold of him straight away, went to him like a lover and rammed my head up into his nose. I had my work cut out, I can tell you that day. We got drunk afterwards together, me and Willie. Big Willie Boswell. I can see 'ee now...'

Nathaniel sealed the cigarette paper with his tongue, and looked at me, the lacquer of age on his dark eyes like the crust of old fires. 'And times could be bad, could be hard. Oh, yes. Hunger, cold, worry. You got to know 'em all.'

He struck a match to his cigarette, his hands cupped around it as if in a gale. 'And I were what they used to call a useful man. I could plough, pack a good straight furrow, sow, reap, mow.' Nathaniel's low, warm breath of a voice blew on the words, rekindling them down the years, coaxingly, with an old confidence.

'I could lay a hedge. Work all day with a scythe. I could lamb, shear, ditch, thatch. Work as a horseman, cowman. Do most carpentry. Do most anything. Yes. That's all gone now, of course. Well, no need for it, see. Noa, no need for it.'

He thought about that for a moment, leaning back with his glass and cigarette, and then said: 'You can't blame they today, though. No. Took near a week then to turn a five-acre field, huddled behind a team of them big old boys, working through whatever the good Lord happened to send down. Now 'tis a morning's work with a tractor, and you can shut yourself up in the cab with a wireless while you'm doing it. Noa, you can't blame they these days.'

Nathaniel took a drink and studied me. 'And I'll tell 'ee something else. You could be out there in winter with nothing in you all the day but maybe a slice or two of fat bacon or a bit of bread and cheese. And your wife at home going without to keep the kids quiet.'

With an old man's sudden anger he went on, 'You had to get out a bit at nights, see! Get out a bit and take some off 'em. Oh, yes!'

Nathaniel turned his face to the fire. 'I had a good old dog then, a lurcher,' he said after a while. 'And an A 410. A poacher's piece. No louder than a sheep's fart.'

He looked up, his eyes gleeful with memory. 'And you could break it in two, see ...' he put down the glass to show me, miming the actions, his hands young again '... tie the butt under one arm, the barrel under the other, and your coat buttoned-up over it. With a new moon on its back, and that old boy of mine slipping ahead ...'

Nathaniel growled with delight. 'My Flora, she'd be up all hours burning the feathers, nagging I out to the back garden to bury the carcasses. The kids hanging out the bedroom window, whispering and giggling, and Flora, holding up the lamp, standing at the kitchen door in her night things.'

He grinned across at me, a brown, cracked grin of teeth, his eyes moist with drink. 'I were a wicked bugger, sometimes, I must tell 'ee that. I were no angel. Noa, no angel.'

We freshened our glasses and drank to that.

It was growing darker in the room now, and Nathaniel, with the aid of his stick, limped over to the light switch, and then drew the curtains.

Returning to his seat, he paused in front of the plaque on the wall, the robin ringed with thorns, and swaying slightly, mock-punched the air in front of it, across the face of it. A gesture which had something in it of the rough, teasing, almost puzzled affection that big men will sometimes show to women and small children. A gesture that speaks not only of strength and weakness, and of experience and innocence. But also, somehow, of wistfulness.

We saw off the last of the cider and Nathaniel got down to the singing. 'The Blackbird',the 'Pleasant and Delightful', and 'The Painful Plough', deftly threading the words through the intricate rhythms, his smoky old voice needing no accompaniment.

'We used to sing a lot in the old days. Sing at work. Sing in the pub. Sing going to work and coming home. Sing to the horses. Sing in the fields. Sing in the sheds. Sing everywhere.'

One of his sons was due to take Nathaniel back with him to spend Christmas with the family, and we mustn't be drunk, noa. But just one, a small one for the road. And because it's Christmas.

Nathaniel lowered his gin and water, and studied me for a few moments, head back, chin pushed out.

And then, as if a challenge, said: 'When I were a lad, father and mother used to tell us that on Christmas Eve, at midnight, the cattle would kneel in their stalls.'

He aimed a sudden forefinger at me. 'Now that were old Christmas Eve, mind. January the fifth. And on Christmas Day, January the sixth, the white thorn, the Holy Thorn of Glastonbury, flowered. The thorn planted by the man who buried Christ. Joseph of Arimathea. Come here to bring the good news. Yes!'

He studied me again, and then smiled, slowly. 'Let you and me have another drink. Another small one. For the road.'

I told him he was a wicked bugger. And he laughed, a sudden shout of a laugh, and slapped his hands together hard, like a horse dealer. 'Yes!' he grinned. 'Yes.'

He saw me to the door after that, standing stiffly and limping his way across. And waited in the doorway until I had reached the gate, the light from it seeing me down the path like a lantern.

There was frost on the air and the smell of fires, the sky quilted with stars. Merry

Christmas and spray-on snow and the lights of trees, and televisions flickering behind drawn curtains as I walked down through the estate.

I took the road which ran along the valley side, and back up into the village, the stiffening fields falling away one side into the night, the glimmerings of lights from scattered farmhouse windows almost drowned in the dark flood of the valley.

And then, walking up into the lampless High Street, the bells of St Mary's broke above me, their simple rough strength shaken from its ancient stone, the full peal ringing out clear across the valley. Ringing out, rising and triumphant, the sound of them in the darkness like the sudden bright comfort of lights.

THE END

Thank you for reading
Under the Apple Boughs

THE BATCH MAGNA SERIES

The first novel in the series, the award-winning The Cuckoos of Batch Magna, and its sequel, Sir Humphrey of Batch Hall, are on Amazon pages: Amazon UK and Amazon US

Peter Maughan is the author of the popular Batch Magna series, published by Farrago Books. His love of the countryside praised in Under the Apple Boughs shines on in the novels, the backdrop to their village setting in a river valley (one Amazon reviewer of the first in the series, The Cuckoos of Batch Magna, considered it to be rather more than a backdrop, that ' landscape in his hands becomes '... a living entity and active participant in the story').

The author lives in the Welsh Marches, the borderland between England and Wales and the setting for the Batch Magna books: http://www.batchmagna.com

FROM AMAZON REVIEWS

"For me, the touchstone comparison is Dylan Thomas's elegiac A Child's Christmas in Wales..."

"It's one of the most outstanding pieces of literature I've ever read. A wonderful collection of non-fiction short stories ... Each story is a stand-alone masterpiece. I absolutely love this collection, and reread it frequently. It restores my faith in the art of fine writing. It's lyrical, descriptive, haunting at times, always beautiful."

Henrietta LaLa (St Martinville, LA)

"A splendid collection of thirteen vignettes of rural life as seen through the eyes of a writer with the soul of a poet. Peter Maughan paints literary landscapes with a Turner palette, all shimmery light, plays of shadows, chiaroscuro and startling detail. The sense of place and the natural flow of the seasons are so strong as to become major actors in his stories while his characters, whether human or animal, stand out in full three-dimensional prominence, illuminated by his compassionate humanity ..."

Angelica Bentley (Dolphin) France, Top 500 Amazon Reviewer.

"... The language and cadence of Peter Maughan's writing is gloriously evocative, and whether one is young or old these little gems of language can be read and re-read with the knowledge that, in his hands, the writing of true literature is not yet on its death bed."

FelicityM, Herefordshire, UK.

"Each story is connected to the other and yet uniquely separate. This book can be read and enjoyed by everyone...man, woman, and child. And as I have said before of his lyrical prose, read it to those who cannot as yet read and I will add now to read it to the elderly for its

music will give solace and comfort ... Peter Maughan, a man for all
seasons, a man whose works will endear him to the ages. All his
writings are classics and have earned a place in world-wide libraries.
They will never be old or outdated...just enjoyed and very loved..every
word...every nuance. Peter Maughan is a gift you give yourself and a
gift for those you love."

Joymarie (United States.)

"I'm already hooked on Peter Maughan's Batch Magna novels but,
even if I weren't, I'd still love this book. Under the Apple Boughs
is literary in all the best ways; lyrical; authentic; and filled with
wonderful descriptions of England's peaceful scenery ... There's the
wonder of unique and powerful imagery. And there's the comfortable
passage of time in a village where people look after each other and
orphaned lambs; where the sea is never too far away, and neither is
winter ... Equally honest in describing the life of robin, badger or man,
the author gently connects all, and connects his readers, with seasons
and land. This is a truly beautiful short trip through a year in the
country, and it's highly recommended."

Sheila Deeth (OR,USA).

" ... Everything they (the other reviewers) say is true; this book, like
Maughan's other work, is charming, sweet, idyllic, lyrical, tender,
poignant and inspiring. I bought this book as soon as it was released,
then held onto it, waiting for the right moment to read it. The right
moment came when circumstances and illness overwhelmed me, and
I knew I needed some cheering up. I dove into Maughan's words,
loving every one, cherishing every one, wishing I could transport
myself to the places of his description but feeling as if, in some way,
I'd already been transported there by the eloquence of the language."

S. Kay Murphy, Vine Voice,(Ontario CA)